GW00733388

FIRST BOOK OF 1
KEYBOARD

Anthony Marks

Designed and illustrated by
Kim Blundell

This book is adapted for electronic keyboard from
The Usborne First Book of the Piano
by John C. Miles

Original music by Barrie Carson Turner,
revised for keyboard by Michael Durnin

Music engraving by Poco Ltd., Letchworth, Herts

Contents

About this book

This book is about learning to play the electronic keyboard. It explains some of the things that electronic keyboard instruments can do and shows you how to read music and play tunes.

As soon as you have learned the first few notes on the keyboard, there are tunes for you to play. Each time you learn something new about music, there is a tune to help you practise it.

For the first tunes, you only need to use one hand at a time. As you get better at playing the keyboard, you can start to use both hands together. This can make playing more interesting.

You will probably have heard many of the tunes in this book already. This can make it easier to play them. You will not recognize some of the others because they have been specially written for this book.

When was the first electric keyboard made? How does the electronic keyboard work? You can find out answers to questions such as these in the book. There are also puzzles for you to try, with answers at the end.

Near the end of the book you can find a whole section full of tunes to play. There are tunes from classical music, Christmas carols, folk songs and duets (pieces to play with a friend).

Getting ready to play

There are many types of electronic keyboard, but most of them work in the same way. These pages introduce you to how they work. The picture shows you some of the things that most keyboards can do.

Electronic keyboards use electricity to make sounds. Before you can play, you must connect your keyboard to an electricity supply. Once you have done this, switch your keyboard on.

Your keyboard might not be exactly like this one. To find out exactly what your own keyboard does, you will have to look at the instruction book that came with it.

Some keyboards use batteries as a supply of electricity. Others have to be plugged in. On some keyboards, you can choose to use batteries or mains.

Most keyboards imitate the sounds of other musical instruments. You have to choose the sound by pressing different buttons.

ON-OFF switch

This is the volume control. It is used to adjust how loudly the keyboard plays.

Some keyboards have an extra volume control for the rhythm section (see opposite).

Keys

Here are the keys. Each one is linked to a musical note. When you press a key, you tell the keyboard which note to play. Find out about keys and notes on page 6.

Most keyboards can play different patterns of drum beats (called rhythms) for you to play along with.

Some keyboards can also add chords automatically to the tunes you play. You need to look at the instruction manual to learn how to do this.

You can find out more about drum beats and chord accompaniments on page 49.

On some keyboards there is a small screen to show you what buttons you have pressed.

Rhythm section

Many keyboards let you record yourself playing, using a device called a sequencer. You can play back the tune you have recorded.

At first it is better if you learn to play tunes without the rhythm section or the automatic chords. Later you can experiment with this feature.

Most keyboards have a button that says "DEMO". If you press it, the keyboard will play by itself to show you some of the sounds it can make.

Some keyboards have a footpedal attached to them to control the volume.

How the keyboard works

The electronic keyboard uses electricity to store sounds and play them back. You tell the keyboard which sounds you want by pressing the keys and switches.

Electricity carries your message along tiny wires inside the keyboard to where the sounds are stored.

In modern electronic keyboards, the part that stores all the sounds is called the microprocessor.

Musical sounds

Music is made from lots of sounds called notes, all put together. On this page and the next, you can find out about the different notes you can play on your keyboard.

At your keyboard

Low sounds

On the keyboard you make high notes by pressing the keys on your right. The keys on your left make low notes.

High sounds

Left. Lower down the keyboard.

Right. Higher up the keyboard.

As you go further down the keyboard to your left, the notes sound lower.

As you go up the keyboard to the right, the notes sound higher.

Play some high notes and some low notes. Use both the black and the white keys. Which keys make the highest notes? Which keys make the lowest notes?

High sounds and low sounds

In music, there is a special word for how high or low a note sounds. The word is pitch. If a note sounds high up, musicians say it has a high pitch. A low note has a low pitch.

The double bass plays low pitches.

The flute plays high pitches.

Notes and their names

All keyboards have the same pattern of keys as the one below. Each key plays a different note, and has a name to go with the note it plays. The keys are arranged in a repeating pattern. The white keys play notes that are named after the first seven letters of the alphabet. As you move up the keyboard on the white keys, the note names go from A to G, then start again from A. In the picture, the white keys have the names of the notes they play written on them.

The first tunes in this book use only the white keys. You can find out about the black keys later on (see pages 32-35).

This key is called Middle C. It is the key that plays C nearest the middle of your keyboard.

Finding the notes

The pattern of the black and white keys will help you to find the different notes. The black keys come in groups of two or three. You can use these groups to work out the position of the other notes on the keyboard.

All the C keys are just below a group of two black keys.

D is always between a set of two black keys.

A is always between the top two of three black keys.

Notes and pitches

Use the picture above to help you find two keys that play the note A. Play them one after the other a few times. Can you hear how the note higher up the keyboard is a higher version of the note lower down? They are different pitches, but they have the same name.

All notes on your keyboard that have the same name are higher and lower versions of each other. Keys that play notes of the same name are always in the same position in the pattern of the keys. The space between two notes of the same name is called an octave.

Play any key, then move upwards step by step to the note an octave above it.

Play each black and white key. How many do you press before you reach the octave?

Whatever note you start on, you will always play seven white keys and five black ones.

You always press twelve keys before you come to the note an octave above the one you started on.

Reading and writing music

On these pages you can find out how to read music so that you can play tunes that other people have made up and written down. You will also be able to write down tunes that you make up yourself. Keyboard music is written on two sets of lines called staves*. Each stave has five lines. The top stave is for notes above Middle C, which are usually played by the right hand. The bottom stave is for notes below Middle C, which are usually played by the left. You can tell the staves apart because of the signs at the beginning of them. The top stave starts with a sign called a treble clef. The bottom one starts with a sign called a bass clef.

Putting notes on the stave

In music dots on the staves tell you which notes to play. The dots are either on the lines or in the spaces between them. Find out more below.

*Some people use the word "staff" instead of stave.

Reading the notes

This page will help you match up the keys on your keyboard with the notes on the staves. At first you may find it difficult to remember everything, but if you practise a little every day it will soon become easier.

The staves below have a picture of a keyboard between them. The notes on the staves are linked by arrows to the keyboard, so that you can see which key plays which note and which note belongs to which key.

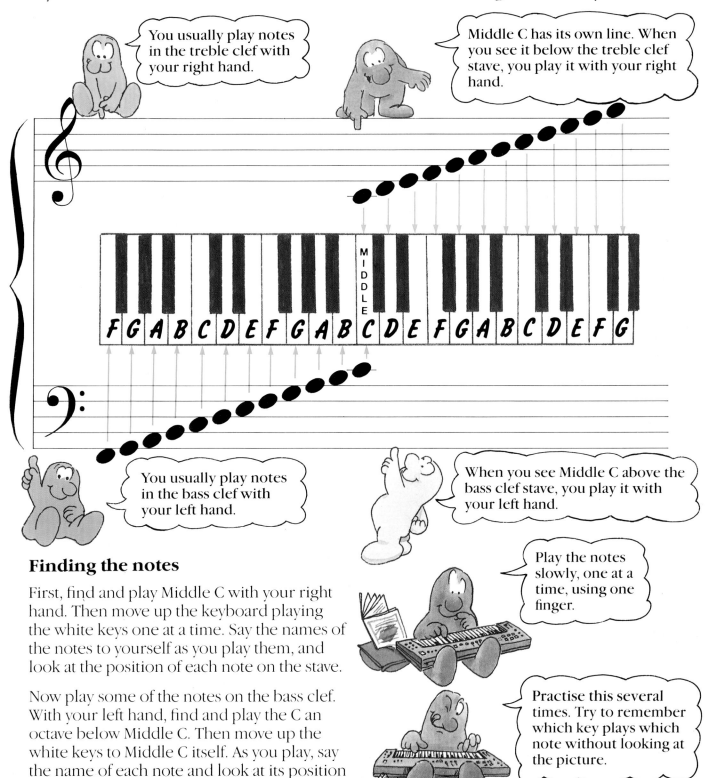

You usually play notes in the treble clef with your right hand.

Middle C has its own line. When you see it below the treble clef stave, you play it with your right hand.

You usually play notes in the bass clef with your left hand.

When you see Middle C above the bass clef stave, you play it with your left hand.

Play the notes slowly, one at a time, using one finger.

Practise this several times. Try to remember which key plays which note without looking at the picture.

Finding the notes

First, find and play Middle C with your right hand. Then move up the keyboard playing the white keys one at a time. Say the names of the notes to yourself as you play them, and look at the position of each note on the stave.

Now play some of the notes on the bass clef. With your left hand, find and play the C an octave below Middle C. Then move up the white keys to Middle C itself. As you play, say the name of each note and look at its position on the stave.

What is rhythm?

A rhythm is a pattern of long and short sounds. Here are some examples of rhythms you can find every day.

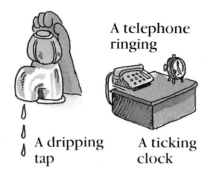

A telephone ringing

A dripping tap

A ticking clock

A horse's hooves

Windscreen wipers

Musical rhythms

Rhythms in music are often based on rhythms in speech. Try saying the words below and see what rhythms they make. You can also clap at the same time.

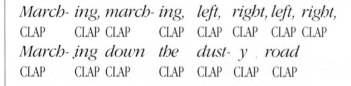

March- ing, march- ing, left, right, left, right, CLAP CLAP CLAP CLAP CLAP CLAP CLAP CLAP *March- ing down the dust- y road* CLAP CLAP CLAP CLAP CLAP CLAP CLAP	*Light-ning ne - ver strikes* CLAP CLAP CLAP CLAP CLAP *In the same place twice* CLAP CLAP CLAP CLAP CLAP

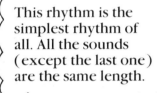

This rhythm is the simplest rhythm of all. All the sounds (except the last one) are the same length.

In this rhythm, some of the claps are slow and some are quick. For instance, as you say "Lightning never" you need four quick claps.

Counting rhythms

Every song or tune has a rhythm. When you play tunes, you cannot clap at the same time. So you count to keep the rhythm steady. (Later in the book you can learn to use your keyboard's automatic rhythm section, if it has one; see page 49.)

Try these simple counting rhythms. Say the numbers a few times, making "One" a little louder than the other numbers. Can you hear how the rhythms of your counting sound different from each other, depending on how many numbers you count?

One, two, one, two,
One, two, one, two,

One, two, three,
One, two, three,
One, two, three,
One, two, three,

One, two, three, four,
One, two, three, four,
One, two, three, four,
One, two, three, four,

This rhythm sounds like a steady march.

This rhythm has a gentle swing to it.

Here is another steady rhythm.

Notes and rhythms

When you write music down, the shapes of the notes tell you which sounds are long and which ones are short. The counts are called beats, and the notes tell you how many beats to make each sound last.

This type of note is called a semibreve or whole note*. It lasts for four beats.

This type of note is called a minim or half note*. It lasts for two beats.

This type of note is called a crotchet or quarter note*. It lasts for one beat.

A rhythm with crotchets

Most of the tunes in the first part of this book have only crotchets in them. To help you practise crotchets, clap this counting rhythm from the opposite page. There is one crotchet for each beat. Can you see how the crotchets fit the rhythm, one for each clap?

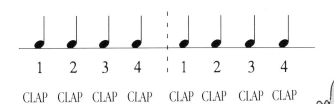

| 1 | 2 | 3 | 4 | 1 | 2 | 3 | 4 |
| CLAP | CLAP | CLAP | CLAP | CLAP | CLAP | CLAP | CLAP |

Writing rhythms down

When music is written down on a stave, the beats are divided into groups called bars. To tell you how many beats there are in each bar, there are numbers at the beginning of a tune, called the time signature. In the music below, the time signature tells you that there are four crotchet beats in each bar. A time signature is a bit like a fraction in maths.

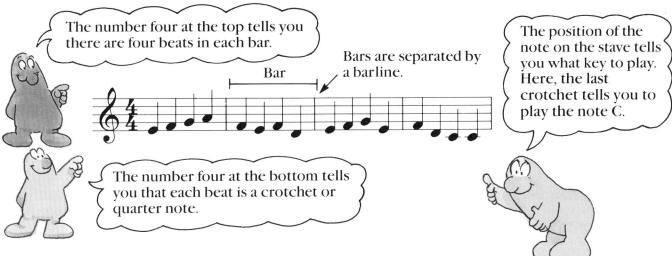

The number four at the top tells you there are four beats in each bar.

Bars are separated by a barline.

Bar

The position of the note on the stave tells you what key to play. Here, the last crotchet tells you to play the note C.

The number four at the bottom tells you that each beat is a crotchet or quarter note.

More time signatures

The time signature below tells you that there are three crotchet beats in each bar.

Can you work out the time signature for this music? (Answer on page 63.)

These are the note names used in North America.

Your first tunes

Here are some tunes for you to try. They use crotchets and the time signatures you found out about on the last two pages.

Here are the keys you will need for the tunes on these pages.

A tune in four-four time

Here is a tune in four-four time. You can use any finger of your right hand to play it. It will help you keep the rhythm steady if you count four to yourself, slowly and steadily, before you begin. Then keep counting quietly to yourself as you play.

Start on Middle C.

Each crotchet lasts for one count.

Practise the tune until you can keep the rhythm steady all the way through. Don't try to play it too fast!

The end of a piece of music always has a double barline. This tells you the piece has finished.

A tune in three-four time

This time signature shows you there are three counts to every bar.

Count "one two three" before you start playing.

A tune in two-four time

This tune is a march. It has two crotchet beats in each bar.

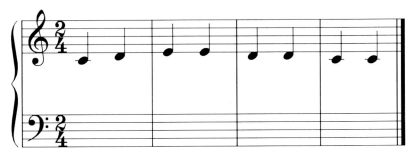

Left-hand tunes

Now try playing this tune with your left hand. Just as the first tune you played went up from Middle C, so this tune goes down from Middle C. It is written in the bass clef.

Right hand

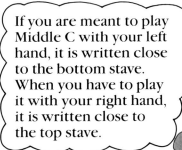

If you are meant to play Middle C with your left hand, it is written close to the bottom stave. When you have to play it with your right hand, it is written close to the top stave.

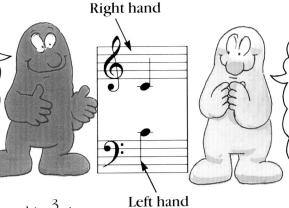

When notes are written above the middle line in either stave, their tails go down. Below the middle line, their tails go up.

Left hand

Here is a tune for the left hand in $\frac{3}{4}$ time.

13

Using different fingers

Here you can find out how to play the notes in a tune more smoothly. As you get better at playing the keyboard, it will also help you to play notes more quickly.

Start by playing the notes C, D and E.

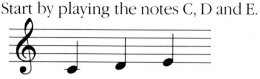

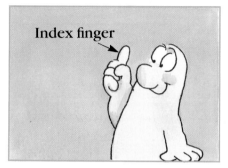

Play these notes one after the other. Use your index finger only. You have to take your finger off each key before you can play the next one.

Now play the same three notes again, using your thumb for Middle C, your index finger for the D and your middle finger for the E.

Press the next key before you have finished taking your finger off the one before. Can you hear how this makes the music smoother?

Finger numbers

Most of the tunes in this book tell you which fingers to use to play the notes. Each tune has numbers in it near the notes. These numbers tell you which fingers to use. The picture below shows you which number stands for which finger.

Every finger has a number.

The little finger on each hand is number 5.

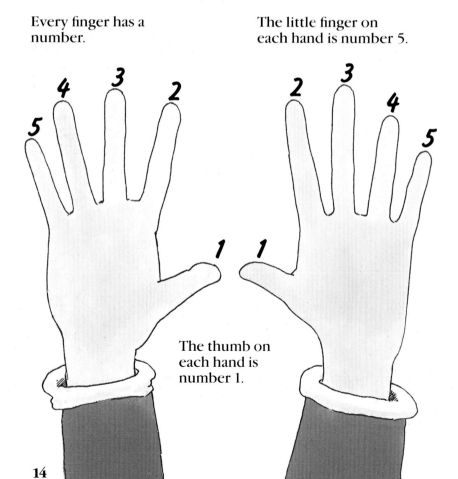

The thumb on each hand is number 1.

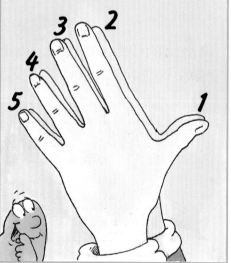

Here is a way to remember which finger has which number. Hold both your hands in front of you, with the palms together. The fingers that touch each other have the same number.

At the keyboard

Now you can begin to practise using all your fingers. This keyboard shows you some keys either side of Middle C. The hands below show you which fingers to put on each key. For many of the tunes in this book, you have to start with your thumbs on Middle C. Don't worry if playing seems difficult at first. Go slowly and it will soon become easier.

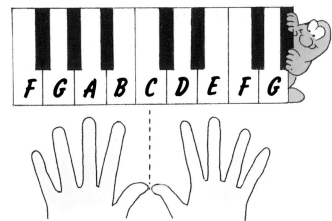

Fingers and keys

Try playing the notes below. Start with the little finger of your left hand (number 5) on the F below Middle C. Now move up the white keys one by one, playing each new key with a new finger. When you reach Middle C, play it twice – once with your left thumb and once with the right. Then continue up the keyboard with the fingers of your right hand, until you reach the G above Middle C with the little finger (number 5).

Now try playing the same thing backwards.

A tune with finger numbers

Here is a tune to play. The numbers tell you which fingers to use for each note.

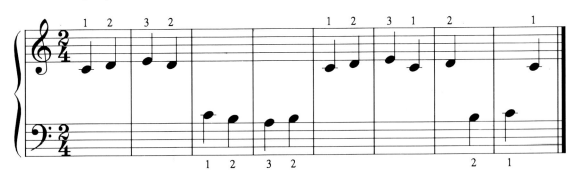

More about rhythms

All the tunes you have played so far have been made up of crotchets (or quarter notes). These are notes that last for one beat. Now you can learn to play tunes with the two longer notes shown on page 11: minims (or half notes) and semibreves (whole notes). On the right there is a reminder about what the notes look like.

A semibreve lasts for four beats.

A minim lasts for two beats.

A crotchet lasts for one beat.

Two minims make up one semibreve.

Four crotchets make a semibreve.

Clapping and counting – semibreves and minims

This rhythm uses the two new notes. Begin by clapping it. Clap once for each note. When you clap a semibreve, you have to wait four counts before you clap the next note. When you clap a minim, you have to wait two counts.

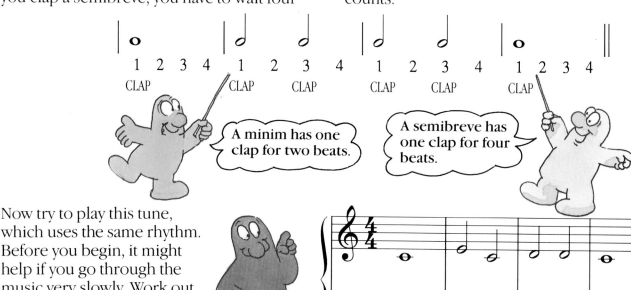

A minim has one clap for two beats.

A semibreve has one clap for four beats.

Now try to play this tune, which uses the same rhythm. Before you begin, it might help if you go through the music very slowly. Work out what the notes are, then fit them to the rhythm you have just clapped.

Keyboard fact

The Telharmonium was one of the first electric keyboard instruments. It was invented in 1906 by an American called Thaddeus Cahill, and was so big that it needed six railway carriages to move it and two people to play it.

The sound came out of a huge horn like this.

Another rhythm

Here is another rhythm to clap. This one starts with a minim. Below it is a tune for your left hand that uses the same rhythm.

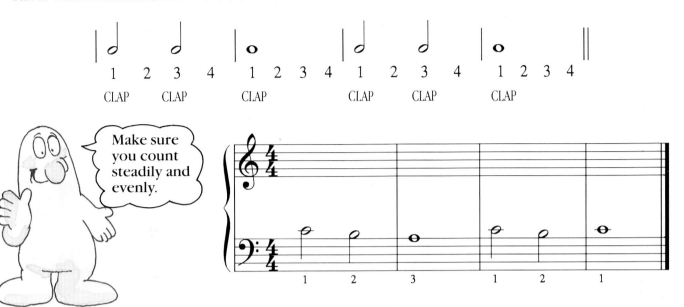

A tune with all the notes together

Here is a tune that uses all the notes you have met so far – crotchets, minims and semibreves. Clap through the rhythm before you start playing.

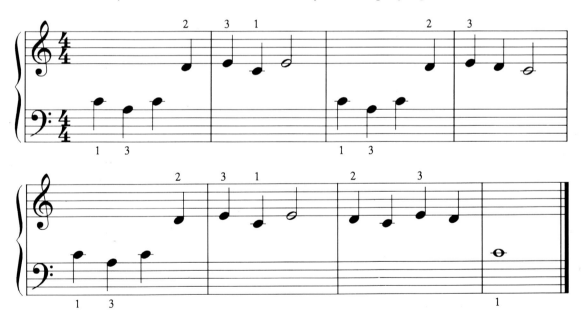

More tunes to play

On the next two pages you will find four tunes to play. There are more pages with tunes later on in the book. As well as being fun to play, the pieces will help you practise the things you have already learned. Don't worry if the music looks difficult at first. Clap, count and play each tune slowly, working out the rhythms and notes as you go.

17

The swallow's goodbye

Desert drums

The circus comes to town

A windy day

Silent beats

Some lines of music have gaps in them where no notes are played. Special signs called rests tell you where to leave a gap. Each rest lasts for a number of beats. Like a note, the shape of a rest tells you how long it lasts. You can find out what rests look like below.

Types of rest

The sign on this stave is a crotchet rest (or quarter-note rest). It tells you to leave a gap of one beat in the music.

This is a minim rest (or half-note rest). Like a minim, it lasts for two beats. You leave a two-beat gap in the music.

This is a semibreve rest (or whole-note rest). You leave a gap of four beats in the music.

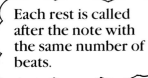

Each rest is called after the note with the same number of beats.

A crotchet note and a crotchet rest both last for one beat.

Counting rests

Clap and count the following rhythm. When you see a rest, say the count but don't clap.

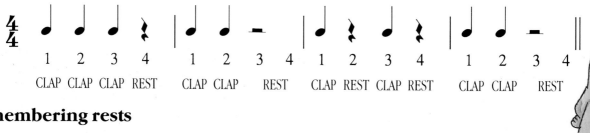

Remembering rests

This chart will help you remember what rests look like and tell you how many beats each one lasts for.

This rest hangs from the line. Think of it as a strong rest that can hang on for four beats.

Think of this rest as a weak one that has to sit on the line. It only lasts for two beats.

Note shape	Rest shape	Count
o	—	4
♩	—	2
♩	𝄽	1

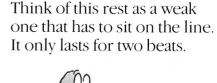

20

A tune with rests

Here is a tune with rests for you to play. Before you begin, clap and count through the rhythm. Leave a gap whenever you see a rest, and say the beats under your breath.

> Don't rush the rests. Count them as if they were notes.

> Whenever the right or left hand plays by itself, the empty bar has a rest in it.

> The semibreve rest tells you to stop playing with your left hand for four beats.

> In the right hand of this bar there is one silent beat.

> Remember to hold the last note for four beats.

New notes

Here are two new notes to add to the ones you have been using.

> This is the position on the stave of the Fs and Gs either side of middle C.

> On the keyboard, F is below any group of three black notes. G is the next white note up.

A tune to play

A semibreve rest is also used to show a whole bar rest, whatever the time signature.

Au clair de la lune

French

Marching tune

Far, far away

Long notes

On this page you will find out about a note that lasts for three beats. On the opposite page you can see how notes can be joined together to make longer notes.

A three-beat note

When you see a dot after a note, it means you have to make it longer by a half as much again. For example, a minim lasts two crotchet beats. A dot adds one crotchet beat to its length.

A minim lasts for two crotchet beats.

A dot adds a half a minim, or one crotchet beat.

Here is a dotted minim. It lasts for three beats.

A tune with dotted minims

Here is a short tune for you to play which uses dotted minims. Make sure that you hold down each dotted minim for three counts.

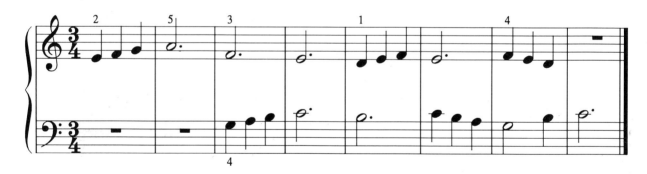

Long sounds on your keyboard

Some sounds on the keyboard last as long as you hold the key down. Others fade quickly. To play long notes, you need to choose long sounds (see page 49). Here are some long sounds you might find on your keyboard.

Pipes

Oboe

Clarinet

Organ

Violin

24

Tying notes together

A note can be made longer by joining it to another on the same line or space. Notes are joined with a curved line called a tie. The new note lasts for the same number of counts as the two separate ones added together.

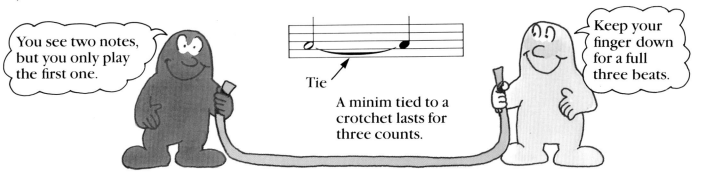

You see two notes, but you only play the first one.

Keep your finger down for a full three beats.

Tie

A minim tied to a crotchet lasts for three counts.

Fill in the boxes

Here are four sets of tied notes. Two have the counts written in. See if you can work out how many counts the other two last for. The answers are on page 63.

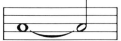

 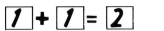 
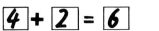

A tune with tied notes

A tied note can cross a barline. Before you play this tune, find all the tied notes and work out how many counts each is worth.

Do not play this note

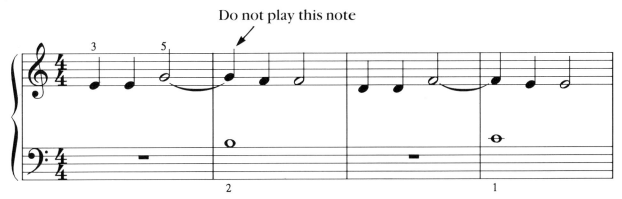

Egyptian dance

Go and tell Aunt Rhody

American

Yankee Doodle

On a swing

Short notes

On these two pages you can learn about some notes that are shorter than a crotchet.

These are called quavers and semiquavers, or eighth and sixteenth notes in North America.

Quavers

A quaver is a note that lasts for half a crotchet beat.

There are eight quavers in a semibreve (whole note).

There are four quavers in a minim (half note).

There are two quavers in a crotchet (quarter note).

Remembering note lengths

Here is a chart to help you to remember how many counts each note is worth. Each line of notes equals four counts.

Think of cutting a cake into eight pieces. It is like dividing a semibreve into eight quavers.

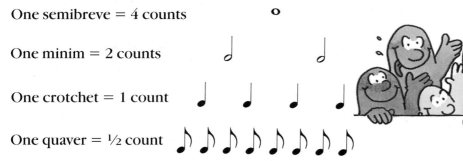

One semibreve = 4 counts

One minim = 2 counts

One crotchet = 1 count

One quaver = ½ count

Joining quavers

In a line of music, groups of two or more quavers have their stems joined together like this:

Clapping and counting quavers

When counting quavers it helps to say "and" for each note after the count. Try clapping and counting these rhythms.

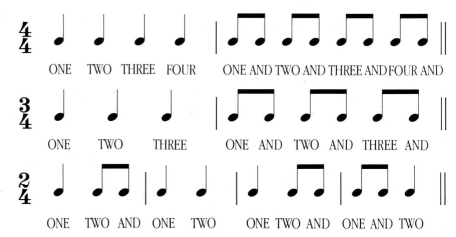

ONE TWO THREE FOUR   ONE AND TWO AND THREE AND FOUR AND

ONE TWO THREE   ONE AND TWO AND THREE AND

ONE TWO AND ONE TWO   ONE TWO AND ONE AND TWO

Semiquavers

A semiquaver (or sixteenth note) looks like a quaver with an extra tail. It lasts a quarter of a crotchet beat.

Two semiquavers are the same length as one quaver.

Like quavers, semiquavers are often joined in groups.

The lines joining quavers and semiquavers are called beams.

Clapping and counting semiquavers

There are four semiquavers in one crotchet beat. You can count groups of four semiquavers as "one-a-and-a". Look at the examples below to see how this works.

A hint

"Semi" means "half of". A semiquaver is half a quaver.

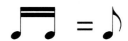

Four semiquavers equal one crotchet. A semiquaver is a quarter of a crotchet. There are 16 semiquavers in a semibreve.

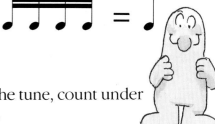

A tune with quavers and semiquavers

Here is a tune to play. Try not to rush – just keep counting steadily, out loud at first.

Once you can play the tune, count under your breath instead.

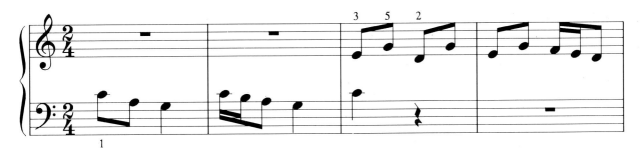

29

Tunes with quavers

On this page are two tunes that use quavers. Before you play, count through each tune and work out the rhythms.

Find out about quavers on page 28.

Hush little baby

American

Starting with part of a bar

Some tunes start with part of a bar. When this happens, the last bar of the tune contains the counts that were not used at the beginning.

Because the first tune below starts on the fourth count, there are only three counts in the final bar.

Count "one, two, three" quietly to yourself. Then start to play on the fourth count.

The last bar has one count missing because the tune started on the fourth count.

Red river valley

American

Dotted crotchets

You can make a note half as long again by adding a dot to it. A minim with a dot is three crotchet beats long (see pages 24-25).

A dotted crotchet is one and a half crotchet beats long.

Half of a crotchet is a quaver.

The dot adds a quaver to the length of the crotchet.

Try clapping and counting this rhythm. The dotted crotchet is followed by a quaver. Clap the quaver on the "and" part of the second beat.

ONE   TWO   THREE FOUR   ONE TWO   AND THREE FOUR

Do not clap on the "two" count in the second bar.

The dotted crotchet is one and a half beats long.

Slow song

Here is a tune that uses dotted crotchets. It will help if you clap and count the rhythm before you start to play.

31

Black keys

So far, you have been using only the white keys on the keyboard. On the next four pages, you can find out about the black keys and how to use them.

Sharps

Sometimes in music you will see a sign that looks like the one on the right written before a note.

A sharp sign is not a note on its own. It always comes in front of a note, on the same line or space as the note to its right.

Sharps make notes higher. A sharp in front of a note means you play the black key nearest to it on the right.

For example, if you see a sharp sign in front of the note F, you play the black key just to the right of the white key that plays F. This key is called F sharp.

Finding sharps

Like the white keys, black keys that play notes of the same name are always in the same position in the pattern of the keys. Here are some examples of sharps and where they are on the keyboard. Try finding and playing them on your own keyboard.

What sharp signs do

A sharp sign makes the note following it into a sharp. If there are any more notes in that bar on the same line or space, they are sharps too.

This is a sharp sign.

This is what sharps look like on the stave.

F sharp is the bottom note in any group of three black keys.

G sharp is always in the middle of a group of three black keys.

D sharp is always the upper black key in a group of two.

A sharp is always the top black key in a group of three.

This note is F sharp.

This note is ordinary F again and not F sharp because it is in a new bar.

This note is also F sharp, because of the sharp sign earlier in the bar.

The effect of the sharp only lasts for one bar.

Key signatures

Some tunes have sharp signs at the beginning, just after the clef symbols. They tell you which notes in the tune must be played as sharps. These sharp signs are called the key signature of the music. On the right you can find out how the key signature works.

Key signature

The key signature tells you to play F sharp instead of F all the way through the tune, in both clefs.

Careful! There are three F sharp notes in this tune.

A tune with sharps

Try playing the following tune. Look out for the sharps!

In this tune the key signature tells you to play F sharp instead of F all the way through the piece.

Handmade music

The Theremin was invented in 1924, and was one of the first successful electronic instruments. It had no keys or buttons to press to play tunes. Instead, it had two aerials, like those on a radio. The player altered the notes by moving his or her hands in front of the aerials.

More about black keys

As well as being called sharps, black keys on the keyboard are sometimes called flats. Flat signs work exactly like sharps (see page 33), but they make notes lower, not higher.

Flats

This is a flat sign. It comes before a note, on the same line or space.

Flats make notes lower. For example, if you see a flat in front of the note B, you play the black key just to the left of the white key that plays B. This note is called B flat. If there are any more B notes in that bar, you make them flats too. After the barline, if there is no flat sign, you go back to playing ordinary B again.

Finding flats

Now find and play these new flats. Remember, on your keyboard the flat note is to the left of the ordinary note. E flat is the black key below the white key that plays E.

A tune with a key signature

Like sharps, flats at the start of a tune are called a key signature. They mean that some notes are flat whenever they appear. In this piece you play B flat all the way through.

Natural signs

This is a natural sign. It always comes in front of a note, on the same line or space as the note to its right.

A natural cancels the effect of a sharp or a flat sign earlier in the bar. Or it can stop the effect of a key signature.

The flat sign makes this note B flat.

This is B natural because of the natural sign.

This note is F sharp because of the key signature.

This note is F natural because the natural sign cancels the key signature in this bar.

Sharps, flats and naturals – a reminder

♯ A sharp sign raises the note.

♭ A flat sign lowers the note.

♮ A natural cancels the effect of a sharp or flat.

A key signature tells you to play one or more notes sharp or flat all through the piece.

A sharp, flat or natural in the middle of a piece is called an accidental.

An accidental only lasts for one bar, or for less if it is cancelled by another one.

A tune to play

Here is a tune with a key signature and accidentals. The key signature means that every B in the piece is a flat. But watch out for the natural sign in the third bar.

35

Scales

Most tunes in this book are based on chains of notes called scales. Scales move step by step up or down the keyboard. There are many types of scale. On your keyboard, the easiest one to play uses only the white notes. It starts and ends on C, and is called C major.

Use this music to help you play C major.

Scales with black keys

You can begin a major scale on any key on the keyboard, but C major is the only one that uses just white keys. If you begin on any other note, you need black keys to make a major scale. Try these scales to find out more.

Start on the F above Middle C, and play each white key until you reach the F above that. Does this scale sound like C major did?

One note in this scale makes it sound different from C major. Listen carefully as you play. Can you work out which note it is?

Try again, but this time play B flat, not B. Now the scale sounds right. It is called F major, because it starts and ends on F.

Now start a scale on the G below Middle C, using only the white keys.

Can you work out where it sounds wrong?

If you make the F in the scale into F sharp, it will sound correct.

This is the scale of G major. It starts and ends on G.

Tones and semitones

A major scale is like a ladder with steps of two different sizes. The small step is called a semitone. The large step is called a tone. To understand this, first play all the keys, black and white, from one C to the next. Follow the red line as you go.

A semitone is the jump from any key to the one directly above or below it (the next black or white key up or down).

D♯ to E is a semitone

C to D is a tone

E to F is a semitone

F♯ to G♯ is a tone

A tone is the gap from any key to the one two jumps above or below it (the black or white key two jumps away).

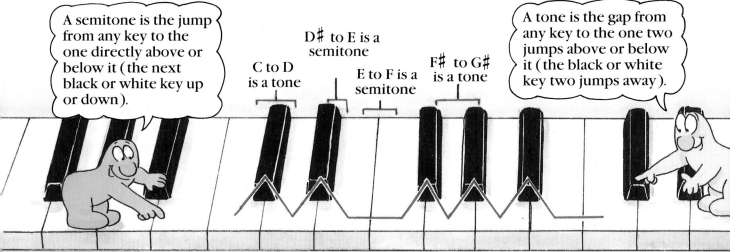

How major scales work

If you play the scale of C major on all the white keys, how big is each jump from one note to the next? Play the scale and measure as you go. Most of the jumps are tones, but two are semitones. Can you work out which they are?

E to F is a semitone

B to C is a semitone

There are eight notes in each octave of a major scale, so there are seven jumps. In every major scale, the seven jumps are always the same, in the same order.

A tone is twice as big as a semitone.

Scales and key signatures

When you tried the scales of G major and F major using only the white notes, they sounded strange because the tones and semitones were in the wrong order. To build a major scale on any key except C, you need to add sharps or flats to make the jumps like those on the ladder above. This is why you need key signatures (see page 33).

A tune that begins and ends on G is usually based on the scale of G major.

It is described as being "in the key of G Major".

You had to play F sharp instead of F natural to make the scale of G major.

Tunes in G major have a key signature to remind you that you need to play F sharp.

You played B flat instead of B natural to make a proper F major scale. A tune based on this scale is "in the key of F major". The key signature tells you that you need to play B flat to make it sound right.

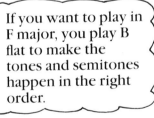

If you want to play in F major, you play B flat to make the tones and semitones happen in the right order.

Black keys and their names

Major scales have either flats or sharps, but never both. In F major, the black key is called B flat, not A sharp. This is because it replaces the note B in the scale of F major. If the black key was called A sharp it would replace the note called A. You need the A in the scale but you don't need B.

The key of G major has F sharp in it. The key signature for a tune in the key of G is F sharp. The black key you play is called F sharp because it replaces the note F in the scale. The black key is not G flat because it does not replace the note G. You need the note G to play the scale.

37

A slow waltz

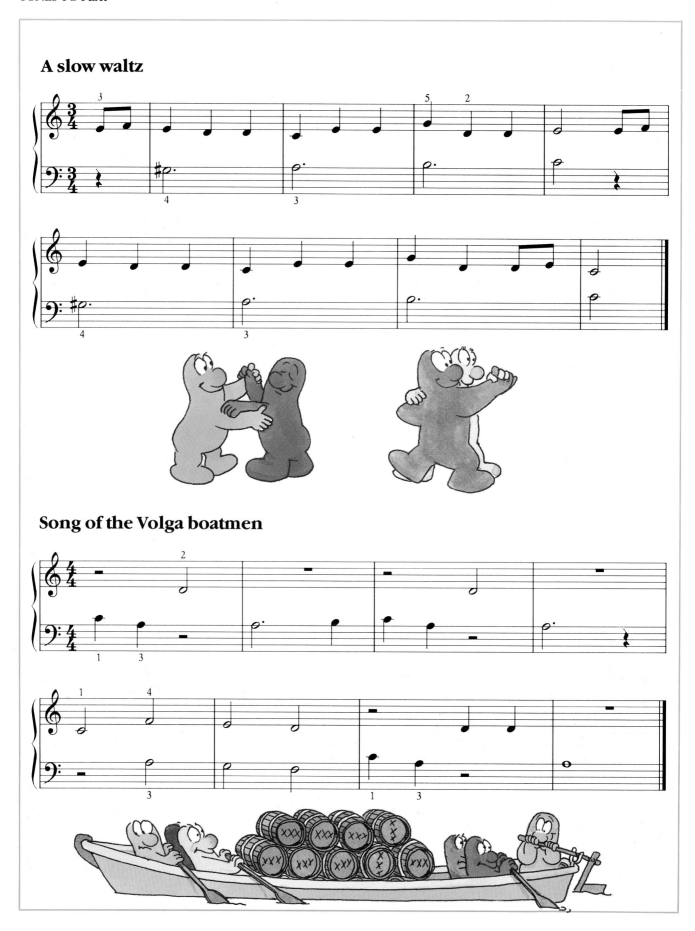

Song of the Volga boatmen

Lightly row

A winter's day

Loud and soft

Some tunes, such as marches, sound best if you play them loudly. Others, like lullabies or sad tunes, sound better played quietly. Sometimes there are signs in the music to tell you how loud or soft to play. The signs are often based on Italian words, because music was first printed in Italy.

The Italian word for soft is *piano*. In music, it is often shortened to **p**.

The Italian word for loud is *forte*. This is sometimes shortened to *f*.

Mezzo is Italian for "quite". *Mezzo-piano* (**mp**) means quite soft.

Mezzo-forte (**mf**) means quite loud.

Sometimes these words end with the letters "issimo", which means "very". *Fortissimo* (**ff**) means very loud.

Pianissimo (**pp**) means very quiet.

Playing loudly and softly

On a piano, and on some large keyboards, the harder you press the keys, the louder the notes sound. But on most electronic instruments you have to find different ways of varying the volume (loudness and softness).

You can adjust the volume control to make the keyboard play louder or softer.

Many keyboards have two separate switches: one for the tune, one for the rhythm (see page 49).

Some keyboards have a footpedal that alters the volume when you press it.

If you want to change the volume in the middle of a tune, you can continue playing with one hand and adjust the switches with the other.

You can alter the volume by choosing loud sounds (like "brass") or soft ones (like "flute").

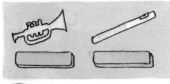

How the piano got its name

Around 1709 an Italian called Cristofori invented one of the first keyboard instruments that could play loudly or softly. He called it a *gravicembalo col piano e forte* ("keyboard with softness and loudness"). This was shortened to pianoforte, and later to piano.

Ragtime capers

River song

Fast and slow

Some tunes sound best when you play them quickly. Others sound better played slowly. Sometimes there are instructions in music to tell you how fast to play. Like the words for loud and soft, they are often Italian. The speed of a tune is called its *tempo*.

If the instruction tells you to play a piece quickly, it means that you have to count the beats quickly. When you play the notes to go with the beats, the music will sound fast. For a slow piece, you count more slowly, leaving longer gaps between the beats.

Allegro means fast or lively. A quick march tune can be played *allegro*.

Lento means slowly. A sad tune could be played *lento*.

Andante means "at a walking pace" – not too fast and not too slow.

Presto means very fast. A happy dance could be played *presto*.

Beats and speeds

As well as Italian words, music sometimes has a different instruction, called a metronome mark. A metronome is a special timing machine for music. Instead of counting beats out loud or in your head, you can use a metronome to beat the time for you. Find out more below.

A metronome can be either clockwork or electronic. It works a like a clock, ticking as each beat goes by.

Your keyboard may have a built-in metronome. Look at the instruction book that came with it.

This is a metronome mark. It is written above the first bar of the music.

MM ♩ = 60

The number tells you how many crotchet beats there are in each minute.

MM stands for Maelzel metronome, after one of the men who invented it.

You set the speed on the metronome using a slider or a dial. The more beats there are in a minute, the faster the tempo.

Metronome speeds

A metronome keeps a steady beat to help you play in time. But it is best to practise pieces without a beat until you can play them well.

If there is a metronome mark at the beginning of a piece, you set the machine to show you how quickly to play. But you can still use a metronome when there is no marking. Here are metronome settings that are roughly the same as the tempo markings described on this page.

Presto	♩ = 96
Allegro	♩ = 84
Andante	♩ = 72
Lento	♩ = 64

In the bleak midwinter

William's march

Repeats in music

Some tunes contain sections that have to be played more than once. Sometimes these parts are not written out twice. Instead there are symbols in the music that tell you to go back and play the section again. This is how some of them work.

Repeat marks

The signs on the right are called repeat marks. They are written on the stave before and after the section that needs to be repeated.

You repeat any music that comes between the two signs.

A tune with repeats

Try this tune. The repeats are explained below.

The first sign shows you where the repeated section begins.

When you reach the second sign, go back to the first one and repeat the section.

When you reach the second sign again, ignore it and play to the end of the tune.

You only play the repeat once, or you could go on playing for ever!

Repeating music from the beginning

Sometimes you repeat part of a tune from the beginning. When you do this, there is often only one repeat mark, with dots on the left-hand side.

Start here.

Play the tune to the repeat mark, then go back to the beginning.

After repeating the first part, play the end of the tune.

Another kind of repeat

There is another sign that tells you to repeat a section. This is the instruction *D.C. al Fine*. The letters *D.C.* stand for *Da capo*, the Italian for "from the top". *Fine* is the Italian for "the end". So *D.C. al Fine* means "go back to the start and play through until you reach the word *Fine*".

Start here and play to the end of the music.

Ignore *Fine* the first time round.

At *D.C. al Fine*, go back to the top and play to the *Fine* mark, where a thick barline shows that the piece has ended.

Fine

D.C. al Fine

Another tune with repeats

Here is a tune with more than one repeat. Look out for the signs.

Allegro

First and second time bars

When a tune contains repeats, it may have a different ending for the first and second time you play it. There are special signs in the music to tell you this.

Play the tune through, including the bar marked 1 (the "first time bar").

When you reach this repeat mark, go back to the first repeat and play the tune again.

When you come to the end of the tune for the second time, ignore the bar marked 1.

Instead, play the bar marked 2 (the "second time bar") to finish the tune.

A tune to practise

Ode to joy

Beethoven

Drink to me only

A new time signature

Here is a new time signature (see page 11) called $\frac{6}{8}$ time. The beats are counted in quavers rather than crotchets, and grouped together in a special way. Do you remember what the top and bottom numbers in a time signature mean?

Johnny Murphy's reel

Here is a tune in $\frac{6}{8}$ time. You need to play it quite quickly so that it swings along. Try to count the two main beats and just "think" the smaller threes.

Sounds and rhythms on your keyboard

Most electronic keyboards can imitate the sounds of other musical instruments. The number of sounds your machine can produce will depend on the make and size of it. Check your instruction manual to find out how the different sounds work.

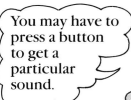

You may have to press a button to get a particular sound.

Or the sound may have a number that you look up on a chart then type in on a keypad.

Choose a sound that goes with the piece you are playing.

For a march tune, try a sound like "trumpet" or "brass".

A slow, quiet tune might sound best played with sounds like "flute" or "violin".

Choosing a rhythm

Most keyboards can play rhythms so that you can have a drum-beat to accompany your tune. You need to look at your manual to see exactly how the rhythms work on your machine. You make the beat faster or slower using a slider or buttons. On some machines the rhythms work like a metronome (see page 42). You type the number of beats per minute on a keypad.

It is best to wait until you can play a piece well before you begin using rhythms.

Listen to the rhythm before you start playing. Does it fit with your music?

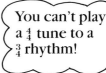

You can't play a $\frac{4}{4}$ tune to a $\frac{3}{4}$ rhythm!

Try the "march" rhythm for a lively piece in $\frac{2}{4}$ time.

Or use the "waltz" setting for a piece in $\frac{3}{4}$ time.

Some keyboards have quite complex rhythms for dances like the samba or the bossa nova.

Automatic chords

Some keyboards also have a feature called "auto-chord" or "one-finger chord". You can set the machine to play different accompaniments to your tunes, but you need to read the instruction book carefully to learn how to do this.

The tunes in this book are to help you learn to play with both hands. So most of the tunes sound better without automatic chords. But you could try using them on "Go and tell Aunt Rhody" (page 26), or "The crocodile's waltz" (page 53).

Legato and *staccato*

Until now, you have been playing notes very smoothly, with no breaks in between. Musicians call this playing *legato*. If there are no signs in the music telling you to play differently, you should play *legato*. Sometimes you will see the word *legato* written on the music.

Some music, however, sounds better if you make the notes quite short and spiky. This is called playing *staccato*. To play *staccato* you hit each key quickly, and take your finger off as soon as you have pressed it.

Short sounds on your keyboard

To play *staccato*, you need to choose sounds on your keyboard that will fade as soon as you take your fingers off the keys. Here are some short sounds you might find on your keyboard.

Harpsichord   Plucked strings   Guitar   Banjo   Harp

Staccato stomp

"From the New World"

Dvořák

Musical sentences

When you speak or write, you organize your thoughts into sentences so that they make sense. In the same way, when people write music down, they organize it into sentences called phrases. A phrase is a section of a tune. Each one is normally made up of a number of bars. A phrase is shown by a long curved line. It connects a group of notes.

Phrase-marks are normally written above the music, like this.

When you play a phrase, you make it sound as if you were singing it all in one breath.

This phrase sounds like a short tune by itself. It starts and ends on F.

A long tune usually has several phrases in it.

At the end of a phrase, lift your hand slightly and make a tiny break before you begin the next one. Think of it as if you were singing and taking a very short breath.

Phrase-marks can look like tie marks (see page 25). But a tie joins two notes on the same line or space. A phrase mark links more than two notes on different lines and spaces.

Questions and answers

When you talk you sometimes use questions and answers. You can do this in music too.

Try playing the music below to see how this works. There are two phrases in this tune.

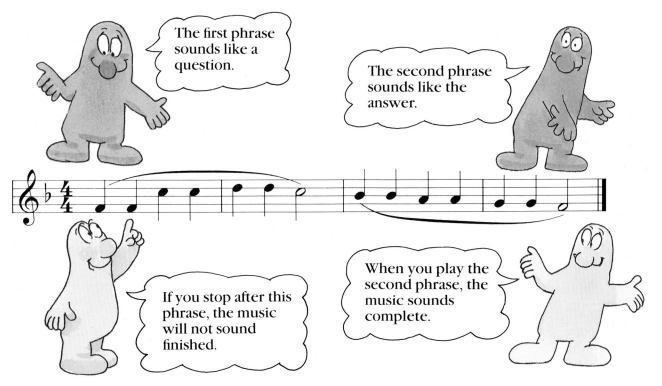

The first phrase sounds like a question.

The second phrase sounds like the answer.

If you stop after this phrase, the music will not sound finished.

When you play the second phrase, the music sounds complete.

The mountain stream

The crocodile's waltz

Lullaby

Kangaroo hop

This old man

She'll be comin' round the mountain

Tunes from classical music

Barcarolle

Offenbach

Fine

D.C. al Fine

Melody in G major

Mozart

Rigadoon

Purcell

Tunes for two players

Here are two tunes for you to play with a friend. You both have to sit at the same keyboard. One person sits on the right and plays part A (the higher notes). The other

person sits on the left and plays part B (the lower notes). It will help if you count one bar together before you begin playing, to help you keep time.

Freight train Part A American

Allegro

Lavender's blue Part A

Andante

Christmas carols

While shepherds watched their flocks by night

Traditional

We three kings of Orient are

Traditional

We wish you a merry Christmas

Allegro

Music words

In this list, you will find explanations of some of the music words used in this book. If a word appears in **bold** type in the text of an entry, that word also has its own entry elsewhere in this list. The words used in North America for notes lengths and other symbols are given in brackets after the main headings.

Accidental.   Any **natural**, **flat** or **sharp** sign that is not part of the **key signature**. The effect of an accidental lasts until the end of the **bar**, or until it is cancelled by another accidental.

Allegro.   Fast or lively.

Andante.   Not too fast; "at a walking pace".

Bar.   A section of music containing the number of **beats** shown in the **time signature**. Each bar in a piece of music is separated from the next one by an upright line called a barline.

Beat.   The unit used to measure the lengths of the notes in a piece of music. Beats make a regular, even pulse and note lengths are measured by counting beats as they go by.

The lower number in a **time signature** tells you what type of beats you have to count. For most of the pieces in this book, the lower number is four, which means that the beats are **crotchets**. So a **minim** lasts two crotchet beats, and a **semibreve** four.

Crotchet (quarter note).   A note that lasts for one count of a 4 bar; a quarter of a **semibreve**. Most of the pieces in this book are counted in crotchet beats, which means that each count is equal to one crotchet.

D.C. al Fine.   An instruction at the end of a piece of music. **D.C.** stands for "*Da capo*", Italian for "from the top". It tells you to go back to the beginning and play the piece again, until you see the word *Fine* ("the end") written below the **stave**.

Dotted note.   A dot to the right of a note makes it half as long again as its original

length. So a dot after a **crotchet** tells you to make it last for an extra **quaver**.

Duet.   A piece for two players.

Eighth note.   *See* **Quaver**.

Flat.   A sign in music that tells you to play a note a **semitone** lower (usually the next black key down the keyboard). Flat signs are either written as **accidentals**, before individual notes, or in a **key signature**, when they affect certain notes all the way through a piece.

Forte (f).   Loud.

Fortissimo (ff).   Very loud.

Half note.   *See* **Minim**.

Key signature.   **Sharps** or **flats** written at the beginning of a piece. They tell you to play certain notes sharp or flat all the way through the music. The effect of a key signature can be cancelled by an **accidental**.

Lento.   Slow.

Legato.   Smooth.

Mezzo-forte (mf).   Quite loud.

Mezzo-piano (mp).   Quite soft.

Middle C.   The key that plays C nearest to the middle of the keyboard. Middle C is written on its own line between the top and bottom staves.

Metronome.   A machine that indicates the **tempo** of a tune by clicking each **beat** as it goes by. Many keyboards have built-in metronomes that let you select the tempo by pressing buttons or switches. On some instruments you can key in the number of beats per minute.

Minim (half note).   A note that lasts for two **crotchet** beats (or half a **semibreve**).

Natural.   A sign that cancels the effect of a **sharp** or **flat** in the key signature. Sometimes a natural cancels the effect of an **accidental** earlier on in the bar.

Phrase. A small section of a tune, like a sentence. You make a small break at the end of each phrase.

Pianissimo (*pp*). Very soft.

Piano (*p*). Soft.

Pitch. How high or low a note sounds in relation to other notes.

Presto. Very fast.

Quarter note. *See* **Crotchet.**

Quaver (eighth note). A note that lasts for half a crotchet beat.

Repeat mark. A sign showing that part or all of a piece of music has to be played more than once.

Rest. A sign that tells you not to play for a certain number of **beats**. In the same way as there are different types of note to tell you how long to play, there are different signs for rests of different lengths.

Rhythm. A pattern of long and short sounds.

Scale. A chain of notes that goes up or down the keyboard by steps.

Semibreve (whole note). A note that lasts for four **crotchet** beats.

Semiquaver (sixteenth note). A note that lasts for a quarter of a **crotchet** beat.

Semitone. The smallest step between two notes on the keyboard. There is a semitone between C and C sharp.

Sequencer. A device on a keyboard that allows you to record music and play it back.

Sharp. A sign in music that tells you to play a note a **semitone** higher (usually the next black key up the keyboard). Sharp signs are either written as **accidentals**, before individual notes, or in a **key signature**, when they affect certain notes all the way through a piece.

Sixteenth note. *See* **Semiquaver.**

Slur. A curved line joining two notes of different **pitch**. To play a slur on the keyboard, play the notes as smoothly as possible.

Staccato. A dot above or below a note which tells you to play the note very short, with a gap before the next note.

Stave (staff). The five lines on which music is written.

Tempo. The speed of a piece of music. There are two kinds of instruction in music to tell you how fast or slow the music should be. Most often there is an Italian word written over the start of the music (*see* **Allegro**; **Andante**; **Lento**; **Presto**). Or there can be a **metronome** marking, telling you how many **beats** there should be in each minute.

Tie. A curved line joining two notes of the same pitch. When you see a tie, you play the first note and hold the key down until the end of the second. Ties are often used to join a note in one bar to a note in the next.

Time signature. Two numbers, one above the other, at the beginning of a piece. The lower one tells you what kind of **beats** to count. The upper one tells you how many beats there are in each **bar**.

Tone. The jump on a keyboard up or down from any key to the key two **semitones** away.

Volume. How loud or soft a sound is in relation to other sounds. You can change the volume of the music by adjusting the volume control on your keyboard.

Whole note. *See* **Semibreve.**

Answers to puzzles

Page 11. There are two crotchet beats in each bar, so this piece of music will have a time signature of ²⁄₄.

Page 25. First set – 3 counts.
Second set – 4 counts.

Index

Foreign musical terms are shown in *italic* type.

Index of tunes

First published in 1992 by Usborne Publishing Ltd, Usborne House, Saffron Hill, London EC1N 8RT, England. Copyright © 1992 Usborne Publishing Ltd. The name Usborne and the device 🎈 are trade marks of Usborne Publishing Ltd. All rights reserved.